D0678296

net.talk

n e t . t a l k

Nancy Tamosaitis

Ziff-Davis Press
Emeryville, California

Editor	Kelly Green
Project Coordinator	Ami Knox
Proofreader	Carol Burbo
Cover Illustration	Dave Feasey and Sarah Ishida
Cover Design	Regan Honda
Book Design	Bruce Lundquist
Illustrations	Dave Feasey and Sarah Ishida
Word Processing	Howard Blechman
Page Layout	Bruce Lundquist

Ziff-Davis Press books are produced on a Macintosh computer system with the following applications: FrameMaker®, Microsoft® Word, QuarkXPress®, Adobe Illustrator®, Adobe Photoshop®, Adobe Streamline™, MacLink® *Plus*, Aldus® FreeHand™, Collage Plus™.

If you have comments or questions or would like to receive a free catalog, call or write:

Ziff-Davis Press
5903 Christie Avenue
Emeryville, CA 94608
1-800-688-0448

ISBN 1-56276-299-0

Manufactured in the United States of America

10 9 8 7 6 5 4 3 2 1

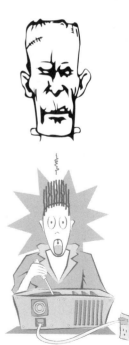

a c k n o w l e d g m e n t s

A GREAT BIG CYBERHUG to my acquisitions editor Eric Stone {{Eric!}}, editor Kelly Green {{Kelly!}}, and assistant editor Margaret Hill {{Margaret!}} for creating both rhyme and reason from the cybercopy submitted! **;)**

Thanks and appreciation to publisher Cindy Hudson for greenlighting the project, and special thanks to Mike Edelhart for recommending me for the gig. **: x**

And to Ron Thompson, forget about our vacation follies because a room with a view is in the dark with you. **ILY.**

INTRODUCTION

1ST THINGS 1ST, netspeak ain't proper writing—in any shape or form whatsoever. Sure, there *are* those Strunk & White diehards on the Net who revel in chastising clumsy prose, bad spelling, or grammatical faux pas with such fervent relish that **IMHO** these folks don't get "lucky" much. Let's make one thing perfectly clear. Netspeak is a combination of casual banter, serious exchange of thoughts and ideologies, and outrageous flirting. Netspeak is conversations you'd have on the phone, group chats with friends at the local corner pub, or even the sorts of debates on social, legal, or civil concerns you'd have at Town Hall. What is important on line is the *message*, not appropriate use of spellcheck. For example, if you're locked in a confessional chat with your girlfriend, you don't suddenly stop her clumsy syntax mid-sentence and shout, "Speak to me in grammatically correct sentences or not at all, dammit!"

You'll notice that netspeak runs rampant throughout the introductory sections of this book. If you're an online **newbie**, you may be confused by the parade of unknown acronyms and emoticons (smileys). If you don't understand what is being said, **RTFM,** *this* manual, because that is what this book is all about. *net.talk* was written to make the digital community fluent in netspeak. It's hard being the new kid on the digital block: Symbols and acronyms come flying by with such unrelenting intensity that newbies and veterans alike often feel left out in the dark. *net.talk* was written to illuminate your personal road on the information superhighway, so that you never face unnecessary detours or insurmountable roadblocks on your digital journey.

Online life today is one enormous global community broken into a seemingly infinite array of small towns. Online devotees revel in meeting people across the world, as well as right across the street, and the dialogue often becomes laden with personal references and hidden meanings. I've communicated with many people on line who I've never had the opportunity to meet **F2F**, but who I feel I know almost as well as my best friend of 26 years.

Online communication is truly "substance over style," as my accomplished friend Philippe Kahn, CEO of Borland International, once wrote to me in e-mail. Physical attributes, whether commonly perceived positively or negatively, hold no ground in cyberspace. Words count. Mental images are formed on the basis of a person's character and intelligence, not by the material droppings of wealth or from the intensity of eye-to-eye physical contact.

IMCO, it is *very* important to differentiate business e-mail from social or recreational sojourns on the information highway. For example, it wouldn't be a kosher business practice to close an e-mail to your boss with a smiley. These days every corporate Tom, Dick, and Harriet is on line and the comingling of netspeak into business e-mail must be done judiciously, if at all. I do admit to throwing the occasional acronym into business-related e-mail. However, I tend to lighten up the tone of business e-mail only if the recipient is someone I know relatively well **IRL**. Adding emoticons to otherwise dry business correspondence can leave recipients with the decided impression that they're dealing with an intellectual lightweight. And throwing in acronyms indiscriminately can leave recipients feeling like they're left out of a secret club. **IAC**, if you have reservations about ending your business correspondence with **:)**, heed your intuition.

SWMBO

OTOH, there are netiquette rules that apply to both social and business situations. One story that comes to mind concerns the aforementioned Mr. Kahn. A former business colleague of mine e-mailed him regarding a business matter. This executive had a disarming but disturbing habit of sending her print and digital memorandums all in capital letters. Kahn replied abruptly, stating, "It is considered bad form to compose e-mail documents in all capital letters. In fact, it translates to shouting on line. Please try and limit your shouting on line to when the occasion warrants." I only know about this correspondence because she was so darn proud of having received a reply from Kahn that she passed the response around the office. However, this story leads us to a simple truth. Typing in all capital letters is a no-no *wherever* you travel digitally. Capital letters can be used for emphasis here and there when you want to convey urgency or a heightened sense of importance. For example, "If we don't follow this course of action today, the company WILL fold this week." No one will chastise you for using a well-placed capitalized word here and there when you have a higher purpose in mind. However, a stream of "I HAVE TO MEET YOU IN PERSON AT COMDEX TO DISCUSS MARKETING YOUR

FORTHCOMING AUTOBIOGRAPHY" will come across as sensitively as a bulldozer on a land mine. Don't do it—EVER! There is nothing worse than an online barker who is constantly **:-(O)**, because it makes unsuspecting readers very **:-t** and **:(**.

Another netiquette guideline that is universally important throughout cyberspace is the old-fashioned virtue of politeness. Civility isn't dead, but it often plays dead on line. **FOS** aside, too many digital devotees become overly empowered by the online medium. **IOW**, many onliners insist on writing nasty, venomous posts directly assaulting another person's character or ideologies. **IMOBO**, I've found that the majority of these **flamers** are meek and mild mannered by day and view flaming as their own special way of retaliating against the lack of power in their daily lives. Having written several online-related books, I've witnessed firsthand the brutal tactics of flamers. For example, recently in a public Internet Usenet forum, I was accused of being male and using a "female facade as a way to sell books." All I can say is kudos to my plastic surgeon. We've really put one over on the general public **;)**. I marvel at the creativity and imagination of these mean-spirited digital dwellers. However, after reading such sci-fi escapades, I log off shaking my head and muttering "Why don't some of these guys **GAL**?"

These flagrant online abuse tactics sometimes even rear their ugly head in business e-mail. I know one administrative assistant who angrily resigned via e-mail. She e-mailed the entire staff of a major entertainment company that her boss, Mr. Corporate, ;-)}<////>, was "a fat, ugly, stupid pig." Even though her words rang with authenticity throughout the company and were silently cheered by many employees, all she ultimately achieved was sabotaging her own career. There is nothing like the feeling of sweet, digital revenge—achieved with the mere touch of the keyboard's Enter key. Living with the consequences, however, isn't nearly as easy. This particular woman came back to work six months later as a temp at a different division of the afore-mentioned entertainment company. The boarlike executive ran into her while she was **GFC**, and immediately had security escort her out of the building.

IME, in general, men and women display vastly different levels of hostility online. Women, as rule, don't flame. The secretary's final hurrah is a different story. The temptation to make a final, grander-than-life **FU** gesture is equally appealing to both sexes. **IMNSHO**, the practice of flaming for flaming's sake is generally a testosterone-induced activity. Throughout my online years, I've received hundreds of flames. Although I've received critical e-mail from women, only men send me blatantly hostile e-mail such as "Don't ever post on this forum again because we all hate you here" or my recent favorite, "I saw you on the *Geraldo* show, and think you're ugly. Redheads repulse me." My internal response is simply **WDUGU** and **DILLIGAF**?

A word to the wise: The best response to flames ignited outside of a work situation is to ignore them, which is the online equivalent of putting out the fire. For a long time, I felt I had to defend whatever unfounded assertions arose on line. No more. If hundreds of digital dwellers really want to think I'm

masquerading as a **MOTOS**, let 'em. People who flame desperately crave attention and live for angry, defensive replies. Take the high road, and let flamers drown in their own sea of social maladaptiveness. **IWBNI** the digital world was less top-heavy with males and the female voice was not so scarce that its presence evoked skepticism in men. Many women are scared off line by the predatory, lascivious tactics of some men. There will be no **m/f** balance to online life if we all don't learn to treat each other with dignity and respect.

Robin Raskin, executive editor of *PC Magazine*, refers to the Internet as "the Wild West of the digital frontier where women are scarce and rules and laws are few and far between." **IMAO**, the online world should live by the same "golden rule" philosophy as **IRL**. **IOW**, if you wouldn't like to read that someone finds you ugly and repulsive as you check your inbox, odds are other people feel similarly.

As you socially traverse through the online universe, I heartily encourage you to incorporate some emoticons and acronyms into your digital vocabulary. You'll find that some emoticons and acronyms are already downright omnipresent, such as the ever-popular **:)** and the frequently used **LOL**. Remember, if someone stops to ask you what a

given emoticon or acronym means, play nice and
refrain from giving off unnecessary **netitude**.
Remember, there was a time when *you too* didn't
know you had to look sideways to understand that
@;^[ ) was Elvis (who is eternally alive in cyberspace, **BTW**) and **@@@@@@@:)** was Marge
Simpson.

WHO'S WHO AND WHAT'S WHAT IN THE ONLINE WORLD

Newbie	Novice onliner, often scorned and derided by veterans
Netitude	Smug attitude emanated by Internet veterans
Flamer	An incendiary onliner who incites trouble by derisive commentary
Flamebait	Something posted publicly that appears designed to inspire flames; usually stated in a way that not only annoys a lot of folks, but also arouses the ire of most readers
Lurker	A digital voyeur who loves to watch but never participates
Netiquette	Behaving in a politically correct manner online, as dictated by the onliners with netitude
Netspeak	Online colloquialisms

"Like I said in the New York Times *on Sunday, 'This business is too important to leave it to the propeller heads.' 8-<:)>"*

—Mark Stahlman, President, New Media Association

SMILEYS

L A U G H T E R

The generic smiley **:)**, without benefit of a nose, or **:-)**, the Jimmy Durante version, are universally welcome wherever one travels socially online. They can be used liberally for punch-line purposes or sprinkled lightly through a message as needed.

:-)	Generic smiley with nose
:)	(or without nose)
:->	Another happy face
:-D	Said with a smile
(-:	Masking theatrical comments
:*)	Clowning around
:-?	Licking lips
%-}	Silly

"The one I use the most often is the plain old :). But I often have to talk about the guy formerly known as Prince. He is now known as 'symbol' but on the Net he's known as 0-+> ;-)"

**—Adam Curry, former DJ for MTV,
now president of On Ramp Inc.**

SARCASM

It is often necessary to spell out sarcasm on line. Too often the written word is interpreted literally, without the sardonic humor that would have been inflected by the human voice.

:/)	Not funny
:-"	Pursing lips
:-r	Bleahhh (sticking tongue out)
:-f	Smirk
:-p	Smirk
:-1	Smirk
:-,	Smirk
:-|	Disgusted
:-J	Tongue-in-cheek comment
:-!	Foot in mouth
:-$	Put your money where your mouth is
:-I	Chewing on a bone

"Re: acronyms and smileys: Here are the main ones I use: :pPpppPpPpP (a raspberry) and)-|==>— (a syringe). I find the rest to be nerdy, but I understand that they are sometimes needed to convey proper intentions. It seems that many people I meet on line are unfamiliar with my sense of humor, so I am not above using a smiley face :) from time to time. I also use 'LOL' to be diplomatic sometimes, but I really hate doing it."

—Mike Saenz, CEO of Reactor (Reactor created Virtual Valerie, the best-selling adult-oriented CD-ROM product)

A N G E R

The good thing about expressing anger on line is that it almost never results in physical injury. Most of us just live too far away from each other to cause any fatalities to one another. Still, be really sure that Mr. Big lives across the continental divide before telling him you'd like to give him a **?-(**.

(:-&	Angry
>:-<	Angry
(:<)	Blabbermouth
?-(	Black eye
%-)	Broken glasses
(:^(	Broken nose
:-t	Cross smiley
:pPpPpP	Giving someone a raspberry
:-p	Left-handed tongue stuck out
:-@	SCREAMING!
:-P	Shouting
:-y	Shouting
:-o	Shouting
:-O	More shouting
:-b	Tongue stuck out
:-(	Unhappy

:-c	Real unhappy
@%&$%&	Venting your spleen (you know what that means…)
@=	Warning about nuclear war

SENTIMENT

A rose is a rose is a rose, even in cyberspace. Only real, live roses beat the cyberthrill of finding a dozen red cyber-roses in one's in-box from a secret (or not-so-secret) admirer. However, cyberkisses *do* leave much to be desired! **;-***

o=	Burning candle to start a flame
-=	Doused candle to end a flame
~=	Flaming message
‖*(	Handshake offered
‖*)	Handshake accepted
[]	Hug
[[*name*]]	Hug
:-x	Kiss

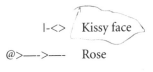

|-<>   Kissy face

@>—->—-   Rose

{{*name*}}   Warm, fuzzy hug

CONSPIRACY

My favorite smiley is the **;)** which I feel is the online equivalent of a knowing wink—for example, posting "Don't worry, your affinity for cross-dressing is a secret safe with me! **;)**"

You may notice that some smileys have more than one meaning. For example, **:-*** is an "oops" in one circle and a "kiss" in another. Just like **IRL**—where, for example, the line between a social and sexual kiss can be gray between new friends—the world of smileys is equally ambigious at times.

     :-#   Censored

     :-T   Keeping a straight face (tight-lipped)

   >:->   Leer

     :-X   Not saying a word

     :-*   Oops! (Covering mouth with hand)

;-) or ;)   Say no more; nudge, nudge

(-_-)   Secret smile

:-8   Talking out both sides of your mouth

'-)   Wink

DESPONDENCY

There is nothing more poignant than the sight of a smiley in pain.
However, use despondent smileys judiciously. Remember, it takes
fewer key strokes to smile than to frown on line!

:-o   "Oh, noooooo!" (à la Mr. Bill)

#:-o   Same as previous

:~/   All mixed up

#-)   Another all-night partier

:-(or :(Boo hoo (sadness)

:-c   Bummed out

:,-(Crying

:~-(Crying

:-e   Disappointed

:-e   Disappointed

:-<   Forlorn

(:-...   Heartbreaking
        message

%-\   Hung over

(:-$	Ill
I-(	Late night message
%+{	Loser in a fight
(:-(	Sad
:-<	Really sad
...—-...	S.O.S.
:-~)	Smiley has a cold
:-'I	Smiley has a cold

A S T O N I S H M E N T

Astonishment in cyberspace is as common as trees in a park—it's everywhere. People revel in showcasing their innermost feelings on line, without worry of **F2F** reality repercussions. For example, two people who just met in cyberspace might proceed to reveal that their secret sexual fantasies include equal parts of flesh, latex, and garden hose. Those same two people meeting off line might *never* have that same conversation.

<:-O	Eeek!
:-o	Shocked
:-C	Unbelievable! (jaw dropped)
:@	WHAT!?
(@ @)	You're kidding!

FILL IN THE BLANK ("YOU'RE A _ _ _ _" OR "I'M A _ _ _ _")

People do a lot of fill-in-the-blanks in cyberspace. Words, not physical imagery, create vivid mental pictures. You're just positive that the woman espousing the Moral Majority viewpoint wears wire-rimmed glasses, sports a bouffant, and favors matronly house dresses, until a **F2F** encounter reveals a Cheryl Ladd lookalike.

O:-)	Angel at heart
(:-)	Bicycle rider, wearing helmet
:-)-{8	Big girl
{0-)	Cyclops
<:-)	Dunce
8:]	Gorilla
<<<<(:-)	Hat salesperson
=:-)	Hosehead
8:-)	Little girl
+<:-|	Monk/nun
-:-)	Mr. T
-:-)	Sporting a mohawk and admiring Mr. T
P-)	Pirate
>< ><	Preppy (wearing argyle socks)
8-<:)>	Propeller head

[:l]	Robot
(-:l:-)	Siamese twins
(:>-<	Thief (HANDS UP!)
<:>==	Turkey

"I do not make use of acronyms or smileys in composing electronic notes. My motto is brevity is the soul of wit—get in, get it, and get out."

—Rush Limbaugh, right-wing radio and TV talk show host

DESCRIBING A MESSAGE

I've met a lot of people in cyberspace who truly read like they've just been ejected from a <:-)<<l but maybe they just don't get out much.

2Bl^2B	About Shakespeare
(O-<	Fishy message
(O—<	Fishy message
(:-lK-	Formal message
:-lK-	Formal message
OO	Turn on your headlights—oblique message forthcoming . . .
:	Message about fuzzy things
*:**	Message about fuzzy things with moustaches

:-#	Message concerning something that shouldn't have been said
<:-)<<I	Message from a space rocket
(:>-<	Message from a cyberthief: HANDS UP!
<{:-)}	Message in a bottle
:-&	Message indicating person is angry
:-$	Message indicating person is ill
<I==I)	On four wheels
<&&>	Rubber chickens (No one minds a rubber chicken in cyberspace—cyber seasonings make all the difference)

FACIAL DISTINCTIONS

If anyone finds a **:-)'** man with **#:-)**, a bad case of **:%)%**, an **:-B** and who **:-w**, please *don't* send him my way!

':-)	Accidentally shaved off one eyebrow
:%)%	Acne
:<)	Attends Ivy League school
´ #:-)	Bad (or matted) hair
:-@	Beard has permanent wave *or* was drawn by Picasso
:^)	Big nose
:>)	Big nose
:-(=)	Big teeth
:-{#}	Braces
|:-)	Bushy eyebrows
:-#	Bushy mustache
%-)	Cross-eyed
&:-)	Curly hair
:-]	Dopey grin
:-)'	Drooling
:-B	Drooling

:	Fuzzy things
*:**	Fuzzy things with beards
8:-)	Glasses on forehead
:<)	Hairy lips
:<)=	Hairy lips and beard, too
:-{	Handlebar mustache
:-=	Hitler mustache
:^)	Large nose
:^{	Mustache
(:-{>	Mustache and beard
:/i	No smoking
.-)	One eye
:-B	Overbite
:-"	Pursed lips
:-V	Shouting
:-W	Shouting with a forked tongue
:~i	Smoking
:~j	Smoking and smiling
:-v	Speaking face profiled from the side

:-w Speaking with a forked tongue

:-O Talking with your mouth full

:=) Two noses

@:-) Wavy hair

ACCOUTREMENTS

On the other hand, there's nothing like a (**:-IK-** man who knows how to wear a (**:)-**), particularly indoors! **;)**

d:-) Baseball fan

:-)8 Bow tie

d :-o Hats off to a great idea!

:-| Playing a harmonica

q:-) To those who wear their hats backwards

8-) Wearing glasses

8:-) Wearing glasses on head

(:)-)	Wearing scuba mask
0-)	Wearing scuba mask
(:-IK-	Well dressed

SMILEY PHRASES

B-)	Got the shades on
:-C	Really bummed out
:-x	My lips are sealed
:-X	My lips are really sealed (or loose lips sink ships)
:-*	Ate a sour pickle
:^(	Nose is out of joint
I-P	Bleahhh
}:-(	Bullheaded
...-...	SOS!
2BI^2B	"To be or not to be"

SMILEY PEOPLE

O:-)	Angel
:-%	Banker
:-)-{8	Big girl

:-)=	Buck-toothed
C=:-)	Chef
;-)}<////>	Corporate-type guy (See the necktie?)
<:-)	Dunce
:-)#	Has a beard
:-%	Has a beard
:-{	Has a mustache
&:-)	Has curly hair
=:-)	Hosehead
(:-)	Is bald
::-)	Is wearing glasses (four-eyes)
8:-)	Little girl
(-:	Left-handed
|^)	New-waver
:-0	Orator
(@@)	Peepin' Tom
:-?	Pipe smoker
+:-)	Priest
=:-)	Punk-rocker
=:-#}	Punk-rocker with a mustache

O-)	Scuba diver
:-[	Vampire

S M I L E Y   A N I M A L S

<:))><	Fish
<+))><	Dead Fish
>`)))>><	Happy Fish
——-<;))><	Caught Fish
<:>==	Turkey
`@;;;;;;;. .	Centipede

"I think smileys and acronyms are a PC crutch for the energy impaired. And like that crutch, the more they are used, the more withered becomes the brain function. Symbols of all kinds should be discouraged. Politicians use them. Preachers use them. And look where that's got us."

—Allan Cole, science fiction and general author, co-author of the bestselling Sten series, author of *The Far Kingdoms*

C E L E B R I T Y   S M I L E Y S

The best thing about being a celebrity smiley in cyberspace is not worrying at all about aging, physical fitness, or death. I hear ratings don't matter much to smileys, either. ;)

=):-)=	Abe Lincoln
~8-)	Alfalfa Smiley

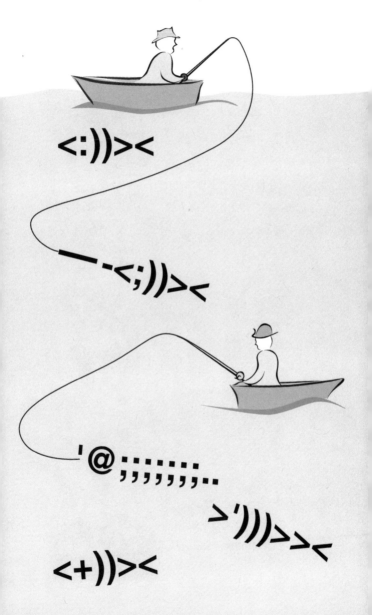

{`   Alfred Hitchcock

{   More Alfred Hitchcock

~8)   Baby Huey

B-)   Batman

*:o)   Bozo

B-,   Bruce Willis (smirking
        dude with sunglasses)

:-{   Count Dracula

===:-D Don King

@;^[)   Elvis

[8-]   Frankenstein

*<(:') Frosty the Snowman

/:-)   Gumby

        Invisible Man

@@@@@@@:) Marge Simpson

B-| Michael Keaton as Batman

%-^   Picasso

0-+>   Prince

7:-)   Ronald Reagan

:-)x   Senator Paul
        Simon

+-(:-)   The Pope

=|:-)=   Uncle Sam

"Sadly, I'm a simple traditionalist who believes that the English language, if utilized properly and with some degree of skill, can express all that need be said on the printed (glass) page."

—James Woods, actor, star of *The Getaway*

MISCELLANEOUS

If you read a message from me stating I **$-)**, you can rest assured that will probably be my last one—I don't know if the phone lines are stable in Tahiti!

:-| "Have an ordinary day" smiley

:-(*)   About to vomit

><><   Argyle socks

:{}   Big mouth (derogatory)

|-O   Birth

[:-]   Blockhead smiley

[:-[Blockhead unsmiley

X:)   Bunny Foo Foo smiley (Nice bow, eh…???)

<:)   Canadian Smiley (Check the toque)

~=   Candle, to denote a flaming message

:-}   Cathy smiley

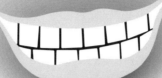

)	Cheshire cat grin
:-)	Comedy
:-8(	Condescending stare
I)	Cyborg smiley
{O-)	Cyclops
O-)	Cyclops (or scuba diver)
*-(	Cyclops poked in the eye
8-#	Dead smiley
:-(	Drama
:*)	Drunk
<:I	Dunce
(:I	Egghead
I"I==={ o~}	Electric guitar
>-	Female

<:-)	For dumb questions (dunce cap)
Q:)	French sailor smiley
O:O	Girl is mooning you
OO	Guy is mooning you
@===(o~)	Guitar
(^-^)	Happy Halloween
:-|	"Have an ordinary day" smiley
|-)	Hee hee
:->	Hey hey
:I	Hmmmm…
|-D	Ho ho
:_)	I used to be a boxer, but it really got my nose out of joint
8	Infinity
:-I	It's something, but I don't know what…
:*)	Jack Frost got smiley
$-)	Just won the lottery
:-*	Kiss
:*	Another kiss

[:]	Kitten smiley in a box as a Christmas present
I-(	Late night message
:-9	Licking his/her chops
:-9	Licking lips
:-	Male
:)	Microhappy
:>	Midget smiley
:<	Midget unsmiley
:-:	Mutant smiley
(-)	Needs a haircut
:~)	Needs a nose job (no explanation necessary)
:-I	No expression face: "That comment doesn't phase me"
:-I	No reaction/Indifferent
:-P	Nyaah! (sticking out one's tongue to the left)

"I used to hate smileys. They seemed too affected and overused. But now I'm a complete convert because I run into too many situations where they're simply the best way to convey a message. My favorite is the smiley with the tongue out :-P. My second favorite is the broad smile :-D. I haven't converted to acronyms yet, but I appreciate when others use them."

—Scott Adams, Cartoonist, "Dilbert"

:-b	Nyaah! (sticking out one's tongue to the right)
[:-=)	Older smiley listening to Walkman radio
:-=)	Older smiley with mustache
.-]	One-eyed smiley
'-)	Only has a left eye, which is closed
(8-)	Owl
#-)	Partied all night
:-\	Popeye
;-\	Popeye gets his lights punched out
:-"	Puckering up for a kiss
=:-#}	Punk-rock smiley with a mustache
=:-(	Punk-rock unsmiley
}:*>	Rudolph the Red Nosed Smiley
:-(	Sad or disappointed face
:-@	Screaming
(:)-)	Scuba diver
(-_-)	Secret smile
:-i	Semismiley
:-/	Skeptical smiley
|-|	Sleeping smiley

#-)	Smashed (from drinking all night)
:-s	Smiley after a BIZARRE comment
>:->	Smiley after a really devilish remark
]:->	Smiley after a really devilish remark
}:>	Smiley after a really devilish remark
:-7	Smiley after a wry statement
:-*	Smiley after eating something bitter
:-6	Smiley after eating something sour, or coughing to one side
:=)	Smiley has two noses
L:)	Smiley in an "Arctic Express" crosswind
8:]	Smiley is a gorilla
:-G-	Smiley is a smoker

:-Q	Smiley is a smoker
I-)	Smiley is asleep (boredom)
P-)	Smiley is getting fresh
(-:	Smiley is left-handed
*<I:-)	Smiley is Santa Claus (Ho Ho Ho)
:-d	Smiley licking its lips
:-9	Smiley licking its lips
+:-)	Smiley priest
:-@	Smiley screaming
:-o	Smiley singing national anthem
:-j	Smiley smiling left
:-?	Smiley smoking a pipe
:-v	Smiley speaking
:-P	Smiley speaking
:-y	Smiley speaking
:-`	Smiley spitting out its chewing tobacco
:-k	Smiley throwing up (or out, depending on your perspective)
:-q	Smiley trying to touch tongue to nose
:-a	Smiley trying to touch tongue to nose
[(:-)	Smiley wearing a toupee

{(:-)   Smiley wearing a toupee

}(:-(Smiley wearing a toupee in the wind

](:-(Smiley wearing a toupee in the wind

[:-)   Smiley wearing a walkman

:-}   Smiley wearing lipstick

;-)   Smiley winking

"I like emoticons and think they should be used in the neXt edition of Strunk and White. As soon as print format books can get the blinking cursor down (a must), then our generation will have made its mark.

Only three emoticons work, however: :) ;) =)

The rest are in the realm of ascii art, which is a cool thing but altogether ego-identification, for example, 8\) (big nose with glasses sorry sensitive guy, etcetera), so, in fact, punctuation can be deconstructed, and the universities that still offer tenure should thank Usenet in the acknowledgement pages of all lit Ph.D dissertations. Especially whichever ivy league conglomerates that in the near future will staff Conde Nast conglomerates. Because the print media rules the electronic media. For now."

—Michael Drinkard, author of *Disobedience*

):-)   Smiley with a big face

(:-)   Smiley with a big face

:-l   Smiley with a bland face

:-#   Smiley with braces

"Yep, I use facial characters all the time. I think it lends another layer of communication online that's really needed. People tend to type in real-time chats as if they were in conversation. That means their thoughts are a bit raw, and facial expressions in a face-to-face conversation would augment the speaker's words, helping with the subtext. So, on line, you can be facetious if you like and people won't get offended if you use a ;) after the statement. Of course, if you're typing a letter to someone, you tend to think through what you're saying a bit more, and buffer your thoughts, explaining them more fully.

Unless you're a 'newbie,' in which case you'll probably go about flaming everyone in real time and in e-mail, having no clue that your electronic words are just as powerful as those spoken face-to-face. I should know. You should see some of the flames I get, especially since my address was published (sheesh).

I tend to use smileys and acronyms only in real-time chats, and tend to use more considered language in e-mail—more in line with the writing of trditional paper mail. But then again, a wink can be very helpful after any devilish comment—even in e-mail. >:)

—Bob West, actor, voice of Barney

    :u)   Smiley with funny-looking left nose

    :n)   Smiley with funny-looking right nose

    {:-)   Smiley with its hair parted in the middle

    }:-)   Smiley with its hair parted in the middle in an updraft

    :-$ Smiley with its mouth wired shut

    :v)   Smiley with left-pointing nose

g-)   Smiley with pince-nez glasses

:^)   Smiley with right-pointing nose

@:I   Smiley with turban

8-)   Smiley with wide-eyed look

(-:   Smiley, left-handed

:) :-) :>   Smiling, happy faces: "Don't take me too seriously"

{:\/   Sounds like a duck (for those "If it looks like a duck and sounds like a duck, it must be a …" situations)

:-'   Spitting

:-"   Spitting out tobacco

:-p)   Sticking tongue out (at you!)

<(^..^)>   Sun with big ears

:-o   Surprised

8-| Suspense

:-v   Talking head smiley <<gab, gab, gab…>>

:-)'   Tends to drool

:-J   Tongue in cheek

:_)   Tongue in cheek

:-P   Tongue stuck out

:-&	Tongue-tied
(l=	Toppled mushroom
:-O	Uh oh
:-o	Uh-oh << gasp >> or ooooh! <<orgasmic>>
:-\	Uncommitted
:-\	Undecided
(:-(	Unsmiley frowning
):-(	Unsmiley with big face
(:-(	Unsmiley with long face
\V/_	Vulcan greeting
:D :-D	Wide happy faces
*!	Wince
;) ;-) ;>	Winking happy faces
o>-<:=	Woman
,-}	Wry and winking
:-z	y.a.c.s.(yet another common smiley)
:-l	y.a.s. (yet another smiley)
:->	y.a.s.
:-(O)	Yelling <<TYPING IN ALL CAPS also = SHOUTING!>>
l-P	Yuk

EXPRESSIONS

<arching eyebrows>

blush

<chuckle>

<falling off the soapbox>

<frown>

<g>

<grin>

"My 'homeroom' online community is the Rocknet forum on CIS, where a group of 30-something music fans that I chum around with tend to regularly use <g> among our witty repartée."

—**Roch Parisien, rock music critic and reviewer**

"I use <g> and BTW on a regular basis."

—**Paul Harris, Radio personality, DC101, Washington, DC**

hug

kiss

<lewd wink>

<making notes…>

<mounting the soapbox>

<raising eyebrows>

<sheepish grin>

<Sheesh!>(tm)

<silly grin>

<smile>

<smiling sweetly>

<smirk>

<wink>

<insert word here>
        Asterisks imply emphasis of a word

"If it's okay with you, I'll pass on making a comment on acronyms and smileys." ;)

—**Tom Clancy, bestselling novelist**

ACRONYMS

G_{ee} I W_{ish} I'd S_{aid} T_{hat}

AA	Alcoholics Anonymous
AAA	Travel club
AAAAA	Travel club for alcoholics
ADN	Any Day Now
AFAIK	As Far As I Know
AFK	Away From Keyboard
ASB	alt.sex.bondage (Usenet newsgroup)

AWGTHTGTTA?
> Are We Going To Have To Go Through This Again?

B4N	Bye for Now
BAD	Broken As Designed
BBM	Big Beautiful Man
BBR	Burnt Beyond Repair
BBS	Bulletin Board System
BBW	Big Beautiful Woman
BIF	Basis In Fact
BIOYIOP	Blow It Out Your I/O Port
BL	Belly Laughing!

BRB   Be Right Back

BRS   Big Red Switch

BTA   But Then Again (in response to IOW)

BTW   By The Way

"As a writer, thus one who values words and how the language is treated, I seldom use acronyms. BTW slips through occasionally, out of laziness. And I've never used a smiley. That's my purist streak showing through, I guess.

But despite how corny and cutesy I think they are, I do use <g> sometimes, although seldom with people who would pick up on my intended meaning easily because we know each other, even if only on line. I learned early on that emoticons can prevent misunderstandings and hurt feelings, and find myself wanting to insert them in earth-mail letters and memos sometimes. (I don't of course.) Psychologists say 70–90 percent of communication is in the body language and tone of voice. We lose that on line, so the gimmicks can help. Yet I've never quite understood why a writer who can convey irony or sarcasm in a published piece can't do the same in online messages. Perhaps it's because they're not long enough to establish tone and context, and because online messages fall somewhere between written and oral communication in style."

—Judith Broadhurst, writer and author

BWQ   Buzz Word Quotient

CU   See you

CUL   See you Later

CUAOP	Cracking Up All Over the Place
CUL8R	See you Later
DIIK	Damned If I Know
DIKU	Do I Know You?? (asked to strangers or people you might know—but aren't sure)
DILLIGAF?	Does It Look Like I Give A F***?
DL or D/L	Download, transmit to you
DTP	DeskTop Publishing
DTRT	Do The Right Thing
DUMKUH	Does Your Momma Know you're Here?? (asked in humor)
DWIMC	Do What I Mean, Correctly
EDT	Eastern Daylight Time
EGADS	Extremely Good Action, Dumb Story (refers to movies)
EOT	End Of Thread (that is, don't reply to this message)
ETLA	Extended Three Letter Acronym
F2F	Face to Face
FA	Fat Admirer
FAQ	Frequently Asked Question
FISH	First In, Still Here
FITB	Fill In The Blank_____

FOAF   Friend Of A Friend

FOS   Freedom Of Speech

FUBAR   F***ed Up Beyond All Repair

FUD   Fear, Uncertainty, and Doubt

FURTB   Full Up Ready To Burst
(about hard-disk drives!)

FWIW   For What It's Worth

FYI   For Your Information

G   Grin (as in <g>)

GAFIA   Get Away From It All
(as in drop out of ILink for a bit)

GAL   Get A Life

gd&r   Grinning, ducking, and running

gd&w   Grinning, ducking, and weaving

GFC   Going For Coffee

GFR   Grim File Reaper (pervasive data destroyer)

GIGO   Garbage In, Garbage Out

GIWIST   Gee, I Wish I'd Said That

GLGH   Good Luck and Good Hunting

GMTA   Great Minds Think Alike

HELP   Handling Energetic Little People
(popular with moms everywhere)

Hir   Gender-neutral pronoun equivalent to
"Him or Her" or possessive pronoun
equivalent to "His or Her"

HNIDWTGP Heck(or H***) No!I Don't Want To Go
Private (for those annoying IMs—instant
messages)

HOYEW	Hanging On Your Every Word!
IAC	In Any Case
IAE	In Any Event
IANAL	I Am Not A Lawyer
IC	I see
IDTT	I'll Drink To That!

IITYWIMIWHTKY
> If I Tell You What It Means,
> I Will Have To Kill You

IITYWIMWYBMAD
> If I Tell You What It Means,
> Will You Buy Me A Drink?

IKWUM	I Know What you Mean!!
ILY	I Love You
IMAO	In My Arrogant Opinion
IMCO	In My Considered Opinion
IME	In My Experience
IMHO	In My Humble Opinion

"I don't use smileys or acronyms because, as a professional writer, I live in horror that these online shortcuts would creep into my work. If people need a reassuring symbol to know how I feel at the end of a sentence, then the sentence, IMHO, hasn't done its job." :)

—Roger Ebert, movie critic, star of "Siskel & Ebert" TV show

"I avoid them all like the plague, except for the basic smiley (which is a very useful invention that can defuse an otherwise harsh line). Maybe we need more punctuation in everyday writing—I've always thought there should be a new mark for a *rhetorical* question, and I'd almost like to see a 'sarcasm' marker.

The reason I don't truck with ROFL and IMHO, etcetera, is that they're too lazy and really are meaningless. IMHO now means 'I'm going to make a stupid plonking comment…' There ain't no such thing as a humble opinion."

—Terry Pratchett, science fiction writer

IMNSHO	In My Not So Humble Opinion
IMO	In My Opinion
IMOBO	In My Own Biased Opinion
INPO	In No Particular Order
IOW	In Other Words
IRL	In Real Life

"I generally use OTOH, BTW, and IRL and that's about it. I think they exist cuz e-mail -is- this strange hybrid between spoken + written conversation, where crummy grammar + spelling are considered OK—where they wouldn't be in other written comms. Anything to minimize the amount of actual typing is considered OK.

As for emoticons, all I use is (grin) as I don't read sideways. Most of the time I can't figure out what they mean anyway. However, I do think they are necessary, if only because e-mail has this strange but well-documented feature where it takes the sardonic, the ironic, and the playful, and turns it into the nasty, snotty, and mean. Why this is, I don't know.

E-mail amplifies disapproval, criticism, and negative emotions in an alarming way. Because of this, I think some kinds of explicit markers are truly required to indicate the tone of the text. (Personally, I often backpedal or get overly explicit to prevent the miscommunication I have encountered with e-mail.)

I use exclamation points a lot more with e-mail than I do with other writing forms. (I don't use them at all in snail mail letters, normal texts, etcetera) '!!!' can often indicate humor and playfulness so that snarky sounding declarations are clearly marked with a kind of exuberance that makes them clearly emblems of (black) (dry) humor, rather than anything else…."

—Paulina Borsook, San Francisco-based writer, frequent contributor to *Wired* magazine and author of *Virtual Romance,* a book-length series of interconnected short stories that delineate how the new information technologies deform relationships

IWBNI	It Would Be Nice If
JIC	Just In Case
JSNM	Just Stark Naked Magic
JTYWTK	Just Thought You Wanted To Know
KMYF	Kiss Me You Fool
KWIM	Know What I Mean?
KWTII	Know What Time It Is? (Is it late?)
L8R	Later
LAB&TYD	Life's A Bitch & Then You Die

LAFS	Love At First Sight
LDR	Long Distance Relationship
LHO	Laughing Head Off!
LJBF	Let's Just Be Friends
LLTA	Lots and Lots of Thunderous Applause
LMAO	Laughing My Ass Off
LO	Lust Object
LOL	Laughing Out Loud

"I use acronyms and emoticons all the time. As soon as I learn a new one, I incorporate it into my computalk. I live to get LOLs." :) Rosie

@>————-/——\———E

—Rosie O'Donnell, comic actress, star of *The Flintstones*

LTNS	Long Time No See
MorF	Male or Female
MEGO	My Eyes Glaze Over
MLA	Multiple Letter Acronym
MOTAS	Member Of The Appropriate Sex
MOTOS	Member Of The Opposite Sex
MOTSS	Member Of The Same Sex

NBIF	No Basis In Fact
NFW	No F***ing Way
NG	Nice Guy/Gal
NSS	No S***, Shylock
NUL	No! You're Lying!
OGKT	Only God Knows That!
OHDH	Old Habits Die Hard

"I never use emoticons. I view them as a crutch which a good writer should not need. Irony, sarcasm and cynicism have been evoked through the written word—sans illustrations—for centuries. There is nothing inherently different about written communication over computer networks which makes it necessary to use emoticons to convey one's message succinctly. That said, the rise in their use seems perfectly logical to me. The smiles and frowns and other hieroglyphics do add a human element to a cyberworld of text—and text alone.

As the technology improves, it seems clear electronic messages will include some of the graphical elements of the written word on paper: distinct fonts, signatures, logos, and letterheads. I suspect as this capability becomes a reality, the use of emoticons to personalize electronic correspondence will diminish.

BTW, I do use digital acronyms on occasion. I started using when I had to tap out e-mail while the CompuServe meter was running OHDH (old habits die hard)."

—Miles O'Brien, Science and technology correspondent,
CNN Atlana

OIC	Oh, I see
OMG	Oh My Gosh! (God!)
OOTC	Obligatory On Topic Comment
OTF	On The Floor
OTOH	On The Other Hand
OTTH	On The Third Hand
OWC	Oh, We See!
P&T	Power & Trust
PABG	Pack A Big Gun
PDA	Public Display of Affection
PITA	Pain In The Ass
PLOKTA	Press Lots Of Keys To Abort
PMBI	Pardon My Butting In
PMFBI	Pardon Me For Butting In
PNCAH	Please No Cussing Allowed Here!!
:::POOF:::	Out of here (Going or signing off now!)
POSSLQ	Person of Opposite Sex Sharing Living Quarters
POV	Point Of View
POW	Problem Older Woman
PTB	Powers That Be

PTMM	Please Tell Me More!
PTUM	Please Tell Us More!
PYM	Problem Younger Man (or Mutant)
PYW	Problem Younger Woman
RE	Regarding
ReHi	Hi again!
RI	Romantic Interest
ROFL	Rolling On Floor Laughing
ROFLAHMS	Rolling On The Floor Laughing And Holding My Side

"ROTFL is my favorite acronym from my early days on line. Interestingly, in my multitude of sexual experiences on line, never has a woman used a digital acronym while we were engaged in heated banter. A lot of women, and a lot of nonshortcutters. I avoid smileys at all costs. My original online signature read 'help stamp out smileys.'"

—Rexxxxxxxx, clandestine author of *Online Sex: Love, Passion and Orgasms on the Sexual Superhighway*

ROMEOS	Retired Old Men Eating Out (popular on SeniorNet)
RP	Romantic Partner
RPG	Role Playing Games
RSN	Real Soon Now
RTFM	Read The F***ing Manual
S/A C	Sex/Age Check
S&M or S/M	Sadism & Masochism, SexMagik
SFLA	Stupid Four Letter Acronym
SGAL	Sheesh! Get A Life!!
SIBU!HH	Sure I believe You! Ha!Ha! (in disbelief)
Sie	Gender-neutral pronoun equivalent to "She or He"
SIG	Special Interest Group
SIWNIMV	Sorry! I Was In IMville! (Popular on AOL)
SMO	Serious Mode On
SMOff	Serious Mode Off
SMOP	Small Matter Of Programming
SMV	Sexual Market Value
SNAG	Sensitive New-Age Guy
SNAFU	Situation Normal: All F***ed Up
SO	Significant Other

"Personally, I'm not much for acronyms or emoticons, although I do have a special place in my heart for homonyms and metaphors. I prefer similes to smileys. I was never much for CB handles either.

Now if you'll excuse me, I have to hook up with FRODO@-basement.com and review the details of last week's 'Babylon 5' episode [SOAWISH] {sort of a wry ironic smile here}"

**—Kevin Murphy, Cast member,
"Mystery Science Theater 3000"**

SOB	Son Of a Bitch
SWMBO	She Who Must Be Obeyed
SYSOP	SYStem OPerator
TAFN	That's All For Now
TANJ	There Ain't No Justice
TANSTAAFL	There Ain't No Such Thing As A Free Lunch
TDM	Too D*** Many
TGIF	Thank God It's Friday
TIA	Thanks In Advance
TTL4N	That's the lot for now
TIATLG	Truly, I Am The Living God
TLA	Three Letter Acronym
TLG	The Living God
TNTL	Trying Not To Laugh!!
TPTB	The Powers That Be

TSR	Terminate and Stay Resident program
TTBOMK	To The Best Of My Knowledge
TTFN	Ta-Ta For Now
TTKSF	Trying To Keep a Straight Face!!
TTL4N	That's The Lot for Now
TTUL	Talk (or Type) To you Later
UAE	Unrecoverable Application Error
UAPITA	You're A PITA
UL or U/L	Upload, send to the BBS
WDUGU	Why Don't you Grow Up!
WFM	Works For Me
WIMP	Windows, Icons, Mouse, Pointing
WOFTAM	Waste Of Flaming Time And Money
WRT	With Regard To
WUF	Where're you From?
WYSIWYG	What You See Is What You Get
WYGIWYPF	What You Get Is What You Pay For
YABA	Yet Another Bloody Acronym

WTGP?   Want To Go Private?

YIU   Yes, I Understand!

YIWGP   Yes! I Will Go Private!

YMMV   Your Mileage May Vary

"On the whole, I find the little symbols a bit tacky, particularly since I frequently speak in double meanings and incorporate irony into my world view. Do you want to see a smiley face at the end of A Modest Proposal? -)?

**—R.U. Sirius, co-founder of *Mondo 2000* magazine,
writer, musician, and multimedia prankster**

ONLINE
SIGNATURES

Opinions expressed here
are probably bizarre.

Usenets soc.singles FAQ defines sig or .sig (signature) as a short, standardized message tacked onto the end of all one's posts. Net signatures usually consist of about four lines of text and frequently include one's e-mail address, home and/or employer's physical address, favority pithy quote, and/or pertinent or impertinent information.

The following signatures are some of the "pithiest" we've found, and reflect a wide array of net personalities.

> "These immigrants are ruining the country!!" — translated from the Iroquois (apologies to Will Durst)

> If you are writing to offer large sums of money, chocolate, fast cars, or other trinkets and amusements, you can try contacting X's inestimable secretary to find X's whereabouts. If you are seeking to serve a subpoena or overdue bill, you've got the wrong address, wrong guy, wrong net, wrong network, wrong planet. So sorry.

> Send me a postcard; get one back!

> "A family's like a gun. You point it in the wrong direction, you're gonna kill somebody." —Martin Donovan as Matthew in Hal Hartley's "Trust"

> MASTER MAIL—Other guys just leave 'em, but I pull up quick to retrieve 'em.

> Speed doesn't kill. Stopping very fast kills.

> It was relatively fast, and a moron could operate it—two big pluses in the online world. — Boardwatch, November 1993

Get back at the IRS, fill out your tax return in roman numerals.

Graffiti I saw on the bus recently: "Wait for me here. —Godot"

Disclaimer: These are my opinions… but others may share them as well.

How seldom we weigh our neighbor in the same balance with ourselves. —Thomas A. Kempis

All I ask is a chance to prove that money can't buy happiness.

A man must be both stupid and uncharitable who believes there is no virtue or truth but on his own side. —Joseph Addison, English essayist and poet (1672–1719)

Disclaimer: An idle mind is the devil's Nintendo!

"I'm called a theoretical physicist because in practice I'm not."

Printed on 100% recycled bits! Help reduce net trash!

Life isn't too short; it's DEATH that's too long…

Opinions expressed here are probably bizarre.

People who live in magnifying-glass houses shouldn't raise ants.

GeeksAreTheMasterRaceGodIsRecursiveCoffeeIsA FoodGroup.

RevoltAwakeAriseShoutYellScreamStruggleDO
SOMETHINGDAMMITMadnessBrillianceCreativi
tyDementiaMathProphesySameS***Different Pile

WhoCaresWhatISayAnyWayKillYourTelevision

Quick Tip #259: Never bet against anyone willing
to wager all of their money in Final Jeopardy on a
topic entitled "Things That are Blue." NOTE:
These thoughts are my own, 'nuff said!

In times of crisis, it is of the utmost importance
not to lose one's head. —M. Antoinette

Hi! I'm a signature virus… copy me to your
signature, pleeeeease.

Two is not equal to three, not even for large values
of two.